"Birchensale" old barn, built with reclaimed monastic timbers

First published in Great Britain in 2004
Copyright © all images Norman Neasom 2004

British Library Cataloguing-in-Publication Data.
A CIP record for this title is available from the British Library.

ISBN 1 84114 392 8

HALSGROVE
Halsgrove House
Lower Moor Way
Tiverton EX16 6SS
T: 01884 243242
F: 01884 243325
e: sales@halsgrove.com
www.halsgrove.com

Produced by Neasom - Brown Associates

Printed and bound in Great Britain by Sprint Print

A pictorial account by Norman Neasom of "Birchensale Farm", the farm where he was born and grew up. Situated on the outskirts of Redditch in Worcestershire, the name "Birchensale" dates back to Roman times and means 'Birches on the Saltway' as the monks from the nearby Bordesley Abbey used to carry the salt from Droitwich back to Bordesley over the land where the farm was later built. It is no longer a working farm and the land that was farmed all those years ago has given away to an expansive development of private housing estates. The old farm house and barn still exist but have been renovated after years of neglect and are now used as a local community centre.

Norman has gained success and recognition as a professional watercolour painter in the intervening years since leaving "Birchensale", but has never forgotten his roots. This account is a fond memory of farming how it used to be in a world very different from the world we live in now.

The shooting party, "Loans Hill"

Dedication

To My Family

Introduction

"Birchensale, Farm Memories in Pictures" have been created from my having been born and brought up on "Birchensale" Farm in the county of Worcestershire. The farm house and old barn are listed buildings, the farm house dating from the early 1700's but the barn is much earlier, a very fine timber building constructed using timbers from the former Bordesley Abbey. The Abbey was given, along with its manors and estates, by Henry V111 at the dissolution, to the Windsor family in lieu of their estate in the south which Henry wanted as a hunting lodge. The Windsors used the ruined abbey as a source of timbers and stone to build farms on their new estate. The Lords Windsor later became the Earls of Plymouth living for a period at Hewell Grange. "Birchensale" and "Loans Hill" were estate farms tenanted by my great grandfather William and "Birchensale" was eventually purchased on the break up of the Hewell estate by my father Joe.

I have named the characters, they were very real and so much a part of my experiences.

Modern farming practices have eliminated so many of the old ways of doing things; hard work but organic!

The Farm Year

Horse Ploughing

Horse Ploughing with "Bowler" and "Flower" in "The Tack Close". "Bowler" had a habit of kicking off his harness if you accidently touched his hind legs!

Muck Spreading

Old Bill Hawlings muck spreading in the "The Tack Close". The farmyard manure from the cowsheds and stables was taken by horse and cart to the fields to be ploughed, spread in heaps across the fields then spread by hand with a four tined fork prior to being ploughed in.

Hand Dressing

A way of patching where a seed drill had missed an area. Fertilisers too could be spread in this way and often were.

Scything

Using a scythe needed skill through experience - the point had a habit of sticking in the ground!

Turning the Hay

Turning hay in "Big Bakers" field to get it dry before carrying. The field behind is "The Cowshed Close" and to the right is "Back Hill".
Should hay still be quite green and damp when ricked it would become very hot and set on fire by spontaneous combustion.

Cutting the Corners

Bill Clark cutting out the corners in "The Tack Close" when starting to harvest a field so that the binder could get round the corners of the field without running over the standing corn, "Birchensale" is in the background on the left. Bill Clark was a World War one veteran.

Shucking or Stooking

Shuckin or stookin the sheaves of corn. After cutting and binding by the harvester. Sheaves were set up vertically in six or eights to keep them as dry as possible until carried. All of this is done by combine harvester now.

Loading "Big Ben"

Loading "Big Ben" a fine old wagon.

Pitching at the Big Barn

Old Bill Hawlings pitching into the big barn on "Birchensale".

The Threshing Machine

The Threshing machine in "Birchensale" rickyard, carrying the chaff to the cowshed to be used in the cow food which they ate whilst being milked.

Counting Sheep

Tending to the Sheeps Feet - or the "Ships fit"

Lowland sheep tended to develop foot rot being a mountain animal.

Shearing The Sheep

The Sheep Wash

The sheep wash at "Birchensale". Situated in the top brook between "Little Bakers" and "Big Bakers" backed by Brockhill Wood. The sheep were washed prior to shearing.

Feeding Time

Sheep are grazers but need extra food at times..

N. NEASOM 1998

Feeding Time

Fetching the Cows up

Fetching the cows up the front hill at "Birchensale" for milking. The cows were milked twice a day, early morning and afternoon.

Milking Time

Hand milking, always milked sat on a three legged milking stool on the right hand side of the cow.

Bringing the Milk Down

Bringing the milk down from the cowshed to the cooler in the farm court.

Collecting the Milk

In the 1930's & 40's Milkman Harold Crow collected milk from "Birchensale" every morning. He smoked a pipe which pervaded the whole farmyard. Milk was ladled out of the churn on the milk float directly into the housewives jug or milk can in the street or on the doorstep, but nobody seemed to catch anything!

The Vet at Calving Time

A difficult birth in the cowshed and Norman Gold the Vet would be called.

Every Day Life

Digging the Farmhouse Garden

Between seasons on the farm when work was slack, father would put the men to dig the large garden at "Birchensale". They resented this and referred to it as "being sent to Purgatory".

Cutting Hay from the Rick

Cutting the hay using a hay knife.

Singling the Roots

Singling the root with a hoe blade approximately 7 - 8 inches long. A gap would be struck in the line of the little root plants leaving a hoe wide gap in between single mangol, turnip or swede plants, it left plenty of room for them to grow to full size. Three weeks would be spent singling and hoeing.

The Mangol Bury

Roots would be stored in a straw based bury like
apples and covered with straw or old hay.

Ditching

Always started digging a ditch at the lowest point where it would be running into a stream or pool and then work uphill.

Rabbiting

Ferrets were put into the rabbit holes to drive the rabbits out where the men with shot guns were waiting.

Father Picking Apples

There was a large orchard at "Loans Hill" Farm and a smaller one at "Birchensale". Apples would be picked in the autumn, some would be stored in the cheeseroom for the families use, the Bramley cooking apples would be buried in a clamp in the garden and taken out at intervals to sell to the greengrocers in the town during the winter, the rest would be pressed to make cider.

Hedge Laying

Should a hedge be allowed to overgrow it will become necessary to lay it. The tall upright members are tapered with a bill hook towards the base until they can be bent down and weaved between hedge stakes driven in a few feet apart. This is done by hand still.

Hedge Brushing

To do this the slash hook needs to be very sharp and is bought up and over the hedge. All done by machine now.

Friday - Pay Night

Father paying the men in the back kitchen at "Birchensale". Back in the 20's and early 30's the wage was a guinea a week.

Fishpool Meadow

In the 1930's, "Fish pool Meadow", a walk to the town in the evening to have a pint and chat up the "birds", Across the meadow from the farm, over the stile into Salters Lane, along left to where it joins Brockhill Lane and Hewell Road under the railway bridge, up Bates Hill into the town centre. Later during the war, crossing the meadow was sometimes difficult on foggy or very dark nights.

The War Years

A Visit from Cousin Hubert

A visit from Cousin Hubert to "Batchley 10 Acres" in his Spitfire. Hubert Palmer, son of Mother's oldest brother William, died in 2001.

Heinkel Bombing the BSA

Early in the war a Heinkel flew over Bordesley where mother was visiting her friend Mrs French. They were in the garden and she recognised it as a German plane with black crosses under the wings. It flew west over "Birchensale" before turning east over Redditch.

There were three 'Bofor' anti aircraft gun implacements on "Birchensale", one on Loans Hill and one at the gas works. The gun crews all watched it without firing until it was over St Stephens church when a great bomb waddled out of it, then the firing started!

The bomb missed the BSA factory, which was making heavy machine guns, and blew three large elm trees out of the ground and left a huge crater, which I understand was later made into a swimming pool.

We heard a rumour that the German plane had come down on the east coast so perhaps the belated AA firing was effective after all.

The Ack - Ack Barrage over Birmingham

The Birmingham anti aircraft barrage fired at approaching German bombers. Time to get behind something, the falling shrapnel was lethal! The red glow was a land mine exploding, so it was said.

Lancaster Bombers Over "Birchensale"

Lancaster 207 Squadron. flying over "Birchensale" from left to right young Bill Hawlings, Old Bill Hawlings and Bill Brewer, "Birchensale" and Redditch are in the background.